# SUSE Linux Enterprise Server 12 - Hardening Guide

A catalogue record for this book is available from the Hong Kong Public Libraries.

Published in Hong Kong by Samurai Media Limited.

Email: info@samuraimedia.org

ISBN 978-988-8406-56-2

# Contents

# About This Guide

The SUSE Linux Enterprise Server Security and Hardening Guide deals with the particulars of installation and set up of a secure SUSE Linux Enterprise Server server and additional post-install processes required to further secure and harden that installation. Security and hardening elements and procedures are best applied to a server both during installation and post-installation and aim to improve the fitness of the system for the purposes demanded by its administrator.

This guide supports administrator in making security related choices and decisions. The individual steps and procedures should be seen as proposals, not as strict rules. You will often need to evaluate the usefulness of measures for your organization yourself.

The objective is to improve the security value of the system. Definitions about the meaning of the term security vary, but we want to settle on one that is both simple and abstract:

*A good system does what it is expected to do, and it does it well.*

*A secure system is a good system that does nothing else.*

The focus of this guide lies on doing "nothing else". The Linux system is constructed in such way that security policies are enforced. These policies consist of the following concepts (fairly generic and incomplete list):

- DAC (Discretionary Access Control): File and directory permissions, as set by `chmod` and `chown`.

- Privileged ports: TCP and UDP ports 0-1023 and raw sockets can only be used by `root`.

- Other privileged operations: Loading kernel modules, configuring network interfaces, all security relevant settings of the Linux kernel. These are operations that can only be done by the root user, that is the user with the user ID 0, or any other process with the necessary capabilities.

Attacking a system means to attempt to overcome (for example, circumvent or break) these privilege boundaries in a way that the administrator of the system or the programmer of the corresponding subsystem has not taken into account.

A hardened system raises the bar by reducing the area that the system exposes to the attacker (often called attack surface). Besides that a hardened system can also provide measures to reduce the impact of vulnerabilities in the parts of the systems that must be exposed to a potential attacker.

Security is about decisions, and whenever security is in (apparent) opposition to function, these decisions become trade-offs. While it can be argued that all systems should be set up to be as securely as possible, some levels of security and hardening may very well be overkill in some cases. Each system's operational environment has its own security requirements derived from business drivers or regulatory compliance mandates. SUSE Linux Enterprise Server can, for example, be configured to comply with security standards, such as SOX, HIPAA and PCIDSS. It can also be set up to fulfill the requirements from the German Federal Office of Information Security (Bundesamt für Sicherheit in der Informationstechnik) as described in BSI TR-02102-1. An effective business requirements analysis should be performed to determine the right level of security and hardening to be applied to a server or defined as part of a baseline server build.

As a final note before we begin: You may encounter individual requirements in regulatory compliance frameworks that may not make sense from a technical perspective, or they do not serve the purpose of improving security. It may be a productive attitude to simply implement what is required, but whenever there is a contradiction to security, an informed discussion in the documentation serves the overall purpose of your regulative compliance framework much more than blindly obeying the specifications. Feel encouraged to dispute list items that you think are counterproductive.

# 1  Assumptions and Scope

References in this document will usually be made to a single server target or host, however the scope can generally be applied to more than one machine. We generally assume that the security target can cover one or more systems running SUSE Linux Enterprise Server.

We explicitly do *not* make any assumptions about the hostility of the network that the systems are connected to, or the cooperative nature of the users that leverage the services provided by the systems.

In turn, this means that you partially define your context on your own when reading through this document. You will need to broaden the meaning of individual portions to adapt it to your environment. In some cases, such as the use case of a server that is exposed to the Internet, this document may even be insufficient or incomplete; however, it may still serve as a good starting point on your journey towards an increased level of confidence that your system will behave like you want it to.

About trust: Trust relationships exist among all systems that participate in networked transactions. In this way, the trust relationship between the people that use the systems is transported across these systems. The chain that is formed by your trust relationships is only as strong as the weakest link. It is good practice to graphically visualize the trust relationships with the services in a schematic overview or map of your network. Generally, it is up to the owner of a resource to enforce the policies imposed on that resource; this would usually be the server that provides the resource. The client that opens a connection to request the resource can only be made responsible for the actions that it performs. This refers to the action of opening the connection to start with, but to nothing else as such.

The case of hostile users is special and unique: The Human Resources department may be able to solve some security problems in your computing environment at least, and some technical measures can. Make sure that the necessary regulations in your environment fit your needs, and that they back your intentions instead of obstructing them if you need to work around a missing support from your HR department (and your management).

Persons that have administrative privileges on a system are automatically considered trusted.

A Linux system—without any additional security frameworks such as SELinux—is a single level security system: From a security policy perspective there is only the superuser (root) and non-privileged users. System users are non-root user IDs that have access to files specific to their purpose. The separation of administrative duties is complicated by this simplicity. Some tools help: Use sudo(8) for administrative tasks, but be aware that after the privilege boundary is crossed, a program running with root privileges does not enforce any file access policies for non-privileged users anymore. vi(1) that runs as root can read and write to any file in the system.

Another tool to mitigate the risk of abuse or accidental misuse of administrative privileges is NetIQ's Privileged User Manager product. More information is available here:

- https://www.netiq.com/products/privileged-user-manager/

Physical security of the server is another assumption made here, where the server is protected from theft and manipulation by unauthorized persons. A common sobering thought among security professionals is the "ten-second Denial of Service": Unplug the wires and reboot the server. Physical security must be ensured and physical access must be controlled. Otherwise, all assumptions about at least the availability of these systems are void.

Note: Cryptography

The use of cryptography to protect the confidentiality of transactions with the services that your system provides is generally encouraged. The need to implement cryptographic enhancements is strongly dependent on the operational environments of all participating systems. Keep in mind that you need to verify all of the possible security benefits that cryptography can provide, for all of your services, and that these benefits are not delivered automatically by turning on the "encrypt" option of your service (if you can enjoy the idyllic situation where encryption is available as a button to check):

**Confidentiality**

Protection against reading the content of a transaction

**Privacy**

Protection against knowing that a transaction exists, and some properties that it may have, such as size, identities of involved parties, their presence, etc.

**Integrity**

Protection against alteration of content. Be aware that cryptography does not automatically provide this kind of protection.

**Authenticity**

Protection against identity fraud. Cryptography that does not know about identities of participating entities cannot deliver this value.

Keep in mind that encryption of data for confidentiality purposes can merely reduce the size of the data to protect from the actual size to the size of the key that is used to encrypt the data. This results in a key exchange problem for encrypted transactions, and in a key management problem for encrypted data storage. Since data is (typically, there are exceptions!) processed in clear, you need your vault unlocked while data within is being worked with. The encryption of such data on the file system or block device layer helps against the theft of the system, but it does not help the confidentiality of the data while the system is running.

If you want to implement a consistent security policy covering multiple hosts on a network then organizational procedures *must* ensure that all those hosts can be trusted and are configured with compatible security configurations enforcing an organization wide security policy. Isolation of groups of systems that maintain data of the same trust domain can provide an adequate means of control; ultimately, the access controls to these systems, both for end users and for other systems, need to be carefully designed, configured, inspected and monitored.

 Important: Trusting Data

Data can only be trusted to the degree that is associated with the domain it comes from. If data leaves the domain in which security policies can be enforced, it should consequently be associated with the trust of the target domain.

For a review of industry best practices on security, the development of sound security processes, controls, development, reviews, audit practices and incident management, you can review a public RFC (request for comments). RFC 2196 is the ongoing work of the world-wide community and individual security and process experts. You can review it online here: http://www.faqs.org/rfcs/rfc2196.html. An RFC is an open and living document that invites comments and review. Enhancements and improvements are welcome; you will find instructions on where to send those suggestions within the document itself.

This guide provides initial guidance on how to set up and secure a SUSE Linux Enterprise Server installation but it is not intended to be the only information required for a system administrator to learn how to operate Linux securely. Assumptions are made within this guide that the reader has knowledge and understanding of operating security principles in general, and of Linux administrative commands and configuration options in particular.

# 2 Contents of this Book

*Part I, "Common Criteria"* contains a reference to Common Criteria and SUSE Linux Enterprise Server. *Part II, "General System Security and Service Protection Methods"* contains more general system security and service protection schemes.

# 3 Available Documentation

We provide HTML and PDF versions of our books in different languages. The following manuals for users and administrators are available for this product:

*Article* "Installation Quick Start"

Lists the system requirements and guides you step-by-step through the installation of SUSE Linux Enterprise Server from DVD, or from an ISO image.

*Book* "Deployment Guide"

Shows how to install single or multiple systems and how to exploit the product inherent capabilities for a deployment infrastructure. Choose from various approaches, ranging from a local installation or a network installation server to a mass deployment using a remote-controlled, highly-customized, and automated installation technique.

*Book* "Administration Guide"

Covers system administration tasks like maintaining, monitoring and customizing an initially installed system.

*Book* "Virtualization Guide"

Describes virtualization technology in general, and introduces libvirt—the unified interface to virtualization—and detailed information on specific hypervisors.

*Book* "Storage Administration Guide"

Provides information about how to manage storage devices on a SUSE Linux Enterprise Server.

*Book* "AutoYaST"

AutoYaST is a system for installing one or more SUSE Linux Enterprise systems automatically and without user intervention, using an AutoYaST profile that contains installation and configuration data. The manual guides you through the basic steps of auto-installation: preparation, installation, and configuration.

*Book* "Security Guide"

Introduces basic concepts of system security, covering both local and network security aspects. Shows how to use the product inherent security software like AppArmor or the auditing system that reliably collects information about any security-relevant events.

Deals with the particulars of installing and setting up a secure SUSE Linux Enterprise Server, and additional post-installation processes required to further secure and harden that installation. Supports the administrator with security-related choices and decisions.

### Book "System Analysis and Tuning Guide"

An administrator's guide for problem detection, resolution and optimization. Find how to inspect and optimize your system by means of monitoring tools and how to efficiently manage resources. Also contains an overview of common problems and solutions and of additional help and documentation resources.

### Book "GNOME User Guide"

Introduces the GNOME desktop of SUSE Linux Enterprise Server. It guides you through using and configuring the desktop and helps you perform key tasks. It is intended mainly for end users who want to make efficient use of GNOME as their default desktop.

Find HTML versions of most product manuals in your installed system under `/usr/share/doc/manual` or in the help centers of your desktop. Find the latest documentation updates at http://www.suse.com/doc where you can download PDF or HTML versions of the manuals for your product.

# 4 Feedback

Several feedback channels are available:

### Bugs and Enhancement Requests

For services and support options available for your product, refer to http://www.suse.com/support/.

To report bugs for a product component, go to https://scc.suse.com/support/requests, log in, and click *Create New*.

### User Comments

We want to hear your comments about and suggestions for this manual and the other documentation included with this product. Use the User Comments feature at the bottom of each page in the online documentation or go to http://www.suse.com/doc/feedback.html and enter your comments there.

**Mail**

For feedback on the documentation of this product, you can also send a mail to `doc-team@suse.de`. Make sure to include the document title, the product version and the publication date of the documentation. To report errors or suggest enhancements, provide a concise description of the problem and refer to the respective section number and page (or URL).

# 5  Documentation Conventions

The following typographical conventions are used in this manual:

- `/etc/passwd`: directory names and file names

- *placeholder*: replace *placeholder* with the actual value

- `PATH`: the environment variable PATH

- **ls**, `--help`: commands, options, and parameters

- `user`: users or groups

- Alt , Alt – F1 : a key to press or a key combination; keys are shown in uppercase as on a keyboard

- *File, File > Save As*: menu items, buttons

- x86_64 This paragraph is only relevant for the x86_64 architecture. The arrows mark the beginning and the end of the text block. ◁
  System z, POWER This paragraph is only relevant for the architectures System z and POWER. The arrows mark the beginning and the end of the text block. ◁

- *Dancing Penguins* (Chapter *Penguins*, ↑Another Manual): This is a reference to a chapter in another manual.

# I Common Criteria

# 1 Overview and rationale

## 1.1 What is the Common Criteria Certification?

Common Criteria is the best known and most widely used methodology to evaluate and measure the security value of an IT product. The methodology aims to be independent, as an independent laboratory conducts the evaluation, which a certification body will certify afterwards. Security Functional Requirements (SFR) are summarized in so-called Protection Profiles (PP), which allows the comparison of security functions of different products if the definition of the Security Target (ST) (which typically uses a reference to the PP if one exists that fits the purpose of the product) and the Evaluation Assurance Levels are comparable.

A clear definition of security in IT products is challenging. Security should be considered a process that never ends, not a static condition that can be met or not. A Common Criteria certificate (below EA7) does not make a clear statement about error proneness of the system (while many of the flaws that exist specifically in operating systems are security-relevant), but it adds an important value to the product that cannot be described with the presence of technology alone: That someone has independently inspected the design of the system in such way that is corresponds to the claims that are made, and that explicit care has been taken in producing and maintaining the product.

The certificate states a degree of maturity of both the product with its security functions and the processes of the company that has designed, built and engineered the product, and that will maintain the product across its life cycle. As such, Common Criteria aims to be fairly holistic with its approach to take everything into account that is relevant for the security of an IT product.

The Evaluation Assurance Level (EAL) shall denote the degree of confidence that the product fulfills the described claims. The levels are from 1 through 7:

- EAL1: Functionally tested

- EAL2: Structurally tested

- EAL3: Methodically tested and checked

- EAL4: Methodically designed, tested and reviewed

- EAL5: Semi-formally designed and tested

- EAL6: Semi-formally verified design and tested

- EAL7: Formally verified design and tested

While EAL1 only provides basic assurance for products to meet security requirements, EAL2 to 4 are medium assurance levels. EAL5-EAL7 describe medium-to-high and high assurance; EAL4 is expected to be the highest level of assurance that a product can have if it has not been designed from the start to achieve a higher level of assurance.

Many commonly known General Purpose/Utility Computing operating systems have been awarded a Common Criteria certificate at EAL4. A "+" after the assurance level denotes an augmentation to the EAL, an addition that is useful for the articulation of security value, but formally not needed at the corresponding EAL.

The SUSE Linux Enterprise Server version 8 was the first Linux system to achieve EAL3+ (Augmentation: Basic Flaw Remediation) in 2003; Version 9 of SLES was the first Linux based operating system to reach EAL4+ in 2004. More certifications and re-certifications have followed targeting SLES 9 and SLES 10-SP1, until the SUSE Linux Enterprise Server version Service Pack 2 was evaluated in 2011/2012.

The Common Criteria evaluations inspect a specific configuration of the product in an evaluated setup. The "Administrator's Guide" is a document that comes with a Common Criteria certified product and describes the individual steps that need to be taken to install and configure the product to a state like it was evaluated.

Very often, the evaluated configuration is used as a reference for the secure installation of the SUSE Linux Enterprise Server. It is however incorrect to understand the evaluated configuration as a hardened configuration: the removal of setuid bits and the prescription of administrative procedures after installation is there to reach a specific configuration that is sane, but this process is clearly insufficient for a hardening claim.

Earlier versions of this document have contained a substantial part that links to Common Criteria evaluated configurations. For clarity and to avoid confusion these chapters have been removed.

Instead, this guide recommends the lecture the documentation that comes with the Common Criteria certificate to understand the Common Criteria evaluation of SUSE Linux Enterprise Server in general, the security functions that are in place within the operating system and how these security functions are relevant for the mitigation of threats. The High Level Design documentation encompasses the design specifics of the SUSE Linux Enterprise Server: Authentication mechanisms, access controls, audit subsystem and system log files, to name a few of them. The accumulated knowledge contained in the documentation allows decision making for hardening purposes at an informed level—find it at http://www.suse.com/security/.

Apart from the valuable documentation that comes with the Common Criteria effort, the following manual pages may be of greater interest to the inclined reader:

"pam(8), pam(5)"

"apparmor(7)" and referred man pages

"rsyslogd(8), syslog(8), syslogd(8)"

"fstab(5), mount(8), losetup(8), cryptsetup(8)"

"haveged(8), random(4)"

"ssh(1), sshd(8), ssh_config(5), sshd_config(5), ssh-agent(1), ssh-add(1), ssh-keygen(1)"

"cron(1), crontab(5), at(1), atd(8)"

"systemctl(1), daemon(7), systemd.unit(5), systemd.special(5), kernel-command-line(7), boot-up(7), systemd.directives"

## 1.2   Generic Guiding Principles

The following guiding principles motivate much of the advice in this guide, and security processes in general, and should also influence any configuration decisions that are not explicitly covered.

**Use Data Encryption Whenever Possible**

> Refer to the *About This Guide* section of this guide. In *Section 1, "Assumptions and Scope"*, the limitations of cryptography are briefly outlined.
>
> Be aware that cryptography is certainly useful, but only for the specific purposes that it is good for. It is not a generic recipe for better security in a system, its use may even impose additional risk on the system. Make informed decisions about the use of cryptography, and feel obliged to have a reason for your decisions, no matter if they are for or against cryptography. A false sense of security can be more harmful than the weakness itself. SUSE Linux Enterprise Server supports encryption for generic network connections (the **openssl** command, **stunnel**), for remote login (**openssh**, **man ssh(1)**), for generic file encryption (**gpg**), for entire file systems at block layer (**dm_crypt**, **cryptsetup**) and for VPN (**iipsec**, **openvpn**).

## Minimal Package Installation

Generally, an RPM software package consists of the package's meta data that is written to the RPM database upon installation, the package's files and directories and scripts that are being executed before and after installation and uninstallation.

If the package does NOT contain

1. setuid- or setgid bits on any of the installed files

2. group- or world-writable files or directories

3. a service that is activated upon installation/activated by default.

then the said package generally does not impose any security risk to the system. Under the above condition, the package is merely a collection of files, and their use shall not be automatically assumed if you do not have any local users on your system. Since the installation of such packages does not have any influence on the security value of the system, the uninstallation of them should not either.

However, a fairly simple reason to keep to a minimal set of packages in your installation is that something that is not present cannot get used. Binaries not installed cannot be executed.

A straight forward way of keeping to a minimal set of packages begins with the installation of the system. You can start the installation of your system by deselecting all packages and then select only those that you want to use. As an example, the selection of the apache2-mod_perl package in YaST would automatically cause all packages to be selected for installation that are needed for the Apache package to operate. Dependencies have often been artificially cut down to be able to handle the system's dependency tree more flexibly. You should be safe if you chose the minimal system, and build the dependency tree from there with your (leaf) package selection.

## Service Isolation—Run Different Services on Separate Systems

Whenever possible, a server should be dedicated to serving exactly one service or application. This limits the number of other services that could be compromised in the event an attacker can successfully exploit a software flaw in one service (assuming that flaw allows access to others).

This point can lead to healthy and robust dialog on system sizing and even further to consolidation or virtualization. The intent with this guidance is to reduce the fault domain and risk where possible.

The use of AppArmor for services that are provided on a system is an effective means of containment. Refer to the AppArmor documentation on your system to learn more. `man apparmor` is a good starting point.

The use of virtualization technology with KVM or with Xen is supported with the SUSE Linux Enterprise Server version 12 SP1. While virtualization is generally designed for server consolidation purposes, its usefulness for service isolation is another good argument. Be aware that the capability of the hypervisor to separate virtual machines is not higher or stronger than the Linux kernel's capability to separate processes and their address spaces. The granularity at which virtualization technology tackles separation may however come with its benefits, being resource-hungry and somewhat clumsy on the other hand.

 Note

Virtualization technology cannot match or substitute the separation strength that is given by running services on different physical machines!

**System fingerprinting and backups**

In the case of the suspicion of an attack against the system, nothing can provide more comfort than

1. a backup

2. a fingerprint of your system to detect modifications

3. having done your homework.

Several tools exist on SUSE Linux Enterprise Server 12 SP1 which can be effectively used for the detection of unknown, but yet successful attacks. These tools come at the cost of relatively little configuration effort, but with the benefit of being able to actually know what has been changed in your system.

In particular, the use of `AIDE` is strongly encouraged. `AIDE`, when run for initialization, creates a hash database of all files in the system that are listed in its configuration file. This allows to verify the integrity of all cataloged files at a later time.

Note

You need to copy the hash database that AIDE creates to a place that is unaccessible for potential attackers. Otherwise, the attacker may modify the integrity database after planting a backdoor, thereby defeating the purpose of the integrity measurement.

Note

An attacker may have planted a backdoor in the kernel. This has an entire variety of consequences: Apart from being very hard to detect, the kernel-based backdoor can effectively remove all traces of the system compromise to the degree that system alterations are almost invisible. By consequence, an integrity check needs to be done from a rescue system (or any other system where an independent system runs, and the target system's file systems are mounted manually).

Note

Security is a lively process. Essentially, in this context, this means that the application of security updates invalidates the integrity database. `rpm -qlv packagename` lists the files that are contained in a package. Generally spoken, the RPM subsystem is very powerful with the data that it maintains, and that is accessible with the `--queryformat` commandline option. A differential update of integrity database with the changed files becomes more manageable with some fine-grained usage of RPM.

A fast and directly accessible backup adds distinct confidence about the integrity of your system and can substitute an integrity check such as described above with AIDE. It is important, though, that the backup mechanism/solution has adequate versioning support so that you can trace changes in the system. As an example: The installation times of packages (`rpm -q --queryformat='%{INSTALLTIME} %{NAME}\n' package name`) must correspond to the changed files in the backup log files.

Note

Make it an integral part of your security routine to verify that your backups work.

# II General System Security and Service Protection Methods

# 2 Introduction

In *Part I, "Common Criteria"* we mentioned the Common Criteria EAL 4+ certified installation and setup that was sponsored by IBM for a select subset of hardware. This certified build is a great first step for customers wanting to build a secure and hardened base system, yet might not address all of the services and software specifics that many customers would be interested in.

This next part will present a more general view and give recommendations and guidance for SUSE Linux Enterprise Server system security. Some topics may seem repeated here (from the previous part) yet the context is very different. More detail will be provided in some sections and certainly some more general examples for a greater number of services.

# 3 Linux Security in General

This portion of the guide will only give basic recommendations instead of strict rules. The procedures and examples here should give you the ability to apply security enhancement techniques to a wider variety of server-based services and programs.

Some subjects of this chapter have been discussed before. However, you will find more details and explanations in this chapter. Selected general topics are:

- Physical Security – Protection of the server from environmental threats (people, places, things).

- Security Policies and Procedures – Server life cycle management, disk/media reclamation, backup and archive security.

- Systems Monitoring – Procedures around event notification/management.

- Systems Automation – Mechanisms and/or procedures for automatic security measures. Heuristics, account control, security reporting and remediation, automated shutdown, etc.

- Systems Management – Methods to obtaining packages, verification and signing keys, patching procedures and recommendations.

- Securing Network – Addition programs, ports and service wrappers – iptables, tcpwrappers, services.

- Remote Access – extra SSH information and key federation. CA integration.

- Common Services – mail, NFS and automount.

- Securing the Kernel and Init Process – parameters, systemd targets, and boot scripts.

- Access Control – user/groups/permissions.

- Password Security and Warnings – Proper setup of passwords, banners and `xinetd`.

- Miscellaneous Security – Assorted security settings and miscellany.

- Resources – Web links, documentation and example references, HOWTOs and general information, product links.

The sections will again be organized by a topical hierarchy for continuity-sake. Refer to the main table of contents for easy reference.

## 3.1 Physical Security

Physical security should be one of the utmost concerns. Linux production servers should be in locked data centers where only people have access that have passed security checks. Depending on the environment and circumstances, you can also consider boot loader passwords.

Additionally, consider questions like:

* Who has direct physical access to the host?

* Of those that do, should they?

* Can the host be protected from tampering and should it be?

The amount of physical security needed on a particular system depends on the situation, and can also vary widely by available funds.

### 3.1.1 System locks

Most server racks in data centers include a locking feature. Usually this will be a hasp/cylinder lock on the front of the rack that allows you to turn an included key to a locked or unlocked position – granting or denying entry. Cage locks can help prevent someone from tampering or stealing devices/media from the servers, or opening the cases and directly manipulating/sabotaging the hardware. Preventing system reboots or the booting from alternate devices is also important (for example CD/DVDs/USB drives/etc.).

Some servers also have case locks. These locks can do different things according to the designs of the system vendor and construction. Many systems are designed to self-disable if attempts are made to open the system without unlocking. Others have device covers that will not let you plug in or unplug keyboards or mice. While locks are sometimes a useful feature, they are usually lower quality and easily defeated by attackers with ill intent.

## 3.2 Locking down the BIOS

 Tip: Secure Boot

This section describes only basic methods to secure the boot process. To fond out more about UEFI and the secure boot feature, see Book "Administration Guide", Chapter 12 "UEFI (Unified Extensible Firmware Interface)", Section 12.1 "Secure Boot".

The BIOS (Basic Input/Output System) is the lowest level of software/firmware that dictates system configuration and low-level hardware. GRUB 2, ELILO and other Linux boot loaders access the BIOS to determine how to boot the host. Other hardware types (POWER/System z) that run Linux also have low-level software/firmware. Typically the BIOS can be configured to help prevent attackers from being able to reboot the host and manipulate the system.

Most BIOS varieties allow the setting of a boot password. While this does not provide a high level of security (a BIOS can be reset, removed or modified – assuming case access), it can be another deterrent.

Many BIOS capabilities have other various security settings – checking with the system vendor, the system documentation or examine the BIOS during a system boot.

 Important: Booting when a BIOS Password is Set

If a system host has been set up with a boot password, the host will not boot up unattended (for example a system reboot, power failure, etc.). This is a trade-off.

## 3.3 Security via the Boot Loaders

The Linux boot loader GRUB 2, which is used by default in SUSE Linux Enterprise Server, can have a boot passwords set. It also provides a password feature, so that only administrators can start the interactive operations (for example editing menu entries and entering the command line interface). If a password is specified, GRUB 2 will disallow any interactive control until you press the key [C] and [E] and enter a correct password.

You can refer to the GRUB 2 man page for examples.

It is very important to keep in mind that when setting these passwords they will need to be remembered! Also, enabling these passwords might merely slow an intrusion, not necessarily prevent it. Again, someone could boot from a removable device, and mount your root partition. If you are using BIOS-level security and a boot loader, it is a good practice to disable the ability to boot from removable devices in your computer's BIOS, and then also password-protecting the BIOS itself.

Also keep in mind that the boot loader configuration files will need to be protected by changing their mode to `600` (read/write for `root` only), or others will be able to read your passwords or hashes!

## 3.4 Verifying Security Action with **seccheck**

It is highly recommended to have scripts in place which can verify that security actions or procedures have been run. Even the best systems administrators can make errors or forget something. If you have a small or large Linux installation or environment, you should consider the use of the **seccheck** scripts.

**seccheck** is the SUSE Security Checker. It is a set of several shell scripts designed to check the local security of the system on a regular basis. There are three main scripts that are executed at different time intervals. They are `security-daily,` `security-weekly` and `security-monthly`. If **seccheck** is not installed on your system, install it with **sudo zypper in seccheck**. These scripts all have schedule entries that get placed in cron that determine when they run. Although cron scheduling is the default behavior, this can be controlled via configuration settings (see next section). The daily script runs at midnight, and if changes are detected since the last run (the night before), an e-mail noting the differences will be sent. The weekly script runs every Monday at 1:00 am, and only if changes to the last run (the week before) are found, a mail with the differences will be sent. The monthly script runs every on every 1st of the month and sends the full last daily and weekly report via e-mail.

### 3.4.1 Seccheck Configuration

Note that you can change the receiver of the seccheck mails from root to anyone else if you add an entry like this one to `/etc/sysconfig/seccheck`:

```
SECCHK_USER="firewall" # exchange firewall is an admin user's account name
```

Also note that the `START_SECCHK` variable from `/etc/sysconfig/seccheck` controls whether the security check will be run from cron. (It is ignored if you call **security-control** manually.) The following daily checks are done:

| `/etc/passwd` check | length/number/contents of fields, accounts with same uid accounts with uid/gid of 0 or 1 beside root and bin |
| --- | --- |
| `/etc/shadow` check | length/number/contents of fields, accounts with no password |
| `/etc/group` check | length/number/contents of fields |
| user root checks | secure umask and `PATH` |
| `/etc/ftpusers` | checks if important system users are put there |
| `/etc/aliases` | checks for mail aliases which execute programs |
| `.rhosts` check | checks if users' `.rhosts` file contain + signs |
| homedirectory | checks if home directories are writable or owned by someone else |
| dot-files check | checks many dot-files in the home directories if they are writable or owned by someone else |
| mailbox check | checks if user mailboxes are owned by user and are readable |
| NFS export check | exports should not be exported globally |
| NFS import check | NFS mounts should have the `nosuid` option set |

| | |
|---|---|
| promisc check | checks if network cards are in promiscuous mode |
| list modules | lists loaded modules |
| list sockets | lists open ports |
| Weekly Checks are as follows: | |
| password check | runs **john** to crack the password file, user will get an e-mail notice to change his password |
| RPM md5 check | checks for changed files via RPM's MD5 checksum feature |
| suid/sgid check | lists all suid and sgid files |
| exec group write | lists all executables which are group/world-writable |
| writable check | lists all files which are world-writable (including executables) |
| device check | lists all devices |

Additional monthly checks are also run, however the key difference is mainly that the monthly file is not a diff like the daily/weekly ones but the full reports in one file.

## 3.4.2 Automatic Logout

The `seccheck` package provides an automatic logout feature. It is a script that runs every 10 minutes and checks both remote or local terminal sessions for inactivity, and terminates them if an idle time is exceeded.

You can configure the functionality in the `/etc/security/autologout.conf` file. Parameters include default idle and logout delay times, and the configuration for limiting maximum idle times specific to users, groups, tty devices and SSH sessions. `/etc/security/autologout.conf` also includes several configuration examples.

Tip

The automatic logout feature is not enabled by default. To enable it, edit `/etc/cron.d/` `autologout` and uncomment the example cron line.

# 3.5   Retiring Linux Servers with Sensitive Data

Security policies usually contain some procedures for the treatment of storage media that is going to be retired or disposed of. Disk and media wipe procedures are frequently prescribed as is complete destruction of the media. You can find several free tools on the Internet. A search of "dod disk wipe utility" will yield several variants. To retire servers with sensitive data, it is important to ensure that data cannot be recovered from the hard disks. To ensure that all traces of data are removed, a wipe utility—such as `scrub`—can be used. Some tools can even be operated from a bootable removable device and remove data according to the U.S. Department of Defense (DoD) standards. Note that many government agencies specify their own standards for data security. Some standards are stronger than others, yet may require more time to implement.

## 3.5.1   scrub: Disk Overwrite Utility

`scrub` overwrites hard disks, files, and other devices with repeating patterns intended to make recovering data from these devices more difficult. It operates in three basic modes: on a character or block device, on a file, or on a directory specified. For more information, set the manual page `man 1 scrub`.

SUPPORTED SCRUB METHODS

**nnsa**

4-pass NNSA Policy Letter NAP-14.1-C (XVI-8) for sanitizing removable and non-removable hard disks, which requires overwriting all locations with a pseudo random pattern twice and then with a known pattern: ran- dom(x2), 0x00, verify.

**dod**

4-pass DoD 5220.22-M section 8-306 procedure (d) for sanitizing removable and non-removable rigid disks which requires overwriting all addressable locations with a character, its complement, a random character, then verify. NOTE: scrub performs the random pass first to make verification easier: random, 0x00, 0xff, verify.

**bsi**

9-pass method recommended by the German Center of Security in Information Technologies (http://www.bsi.bund.de): 0xff, 0xfe, 0xfd, 0xfb, 0xf7, 0xef, 0xdf, 0xbf, 0x7f.

**gutmann**

The canonical 35-pass sequence described in Gutmann's paper cited below.

**schneier**

7-pass method described by Bruce Schneier in "Applied Cryptography" (1996): 0x00, 0xff, random(x5)

**pfitzner7**

Roy Pfitzner's 7-random-pass method: random(x7).

**pfitzner33**

Roy Pfitzner's 33-random-pass method: random(x33).

**usarmy**

US Army AR380-19 method: 0x00, 0xff, random. (Note: identical to DoD 522.22-M section 8-306 procedure (e) for sanitizing magnetic core memory).

**fillzero**

1-pass pattern: 0x00.

**fillff**

1-pass pattern: 0xff.

**random**

1-pass pattern: random(x1).

**random2**

2-pass pattern: random(x2).

**old**

6-pass pre-version 1.7 scrub method: 0x00, 0xff, 0xaa, 0x00, 0x55, verify.

**fastold**

5-pass pattern: 0x00, 0xff, 0xaa, 0x55, verify.

**custom=string**

1-pass custom pattern. String may contain C-style numerical escapes: \nnn (octal) or \xnn (hex).

## 3.6  Backups

If your system is compromised, backups can be used to restore a prior system state. When bugs or accidents occur, backups can also be used to compare the current system against an older version. For production systems, it is very important to take some backups off-site for cases like disasters (for example off-site storage of tapes/recordable media, or off-site initiated).

For legal reasons, some firms and organizations must be careful about backing up too much information and holding it too long. If your environment has a policy regarding the destruction of old paper files, you might need to extend this policy to Linux backup tapes as well.

## 3.7  Disk Partitions

Servers should have separate file systems for at least `/`, `/boot`, `/usr`, `/var`, `/tmp`, and `/home`. You do not want that for example logging and temporary space under `/var` and `/tmp` fill up the root partition. Third-party applications should be on separate file systems as well, for example under `/opt`.

You are advised to review *Part I, "Common Criteria"*. It is important to understand the need to separate the partitions that could impact a running system (for example, log files filling up `/var/log` are a good reason to separate `/var` from the `/` partition). Another thing to keep in mind is that you will likely need to leverage LVM or another volume manager or at the very least the extended partition type to work around the limitations of primary partitions (4 partitions).

Another capability in SUSE Linux Enterprise Server is encrypting a partition or even a single directory or file as a container. Refer to *Book "Security Guide", Chapter 11 "Encrypting Partitions and Files"* for details.

## 3.8  Firewall (iptables)

iptables will not be covered in detail in this guide. Most companies use dedicated firewalls or appliances to protect their servers in a production network. This is strongly recommended for secure environments. SUSE Linux Enterprise Server also includes SuSEFirewall2 which is a wrapper for iptables and is enabled by default as a simple and layered protection.

If you are also interested in Linux stateful firewalls using iptables, there are many guides on the Internet. See the Appendix for resources. For lots of iptables tutorials and examples, see http://www.linuxguruz.com/iptables/.

## 3.9  Security Features in the Kernel

The following list shows tunable kernel parameters you can use to secure your Linux server against attacks. Some are defaults already within the SLE distributions. To check the current status of any of these settings, you can query the kernel (`/proc/sys/...` contents). For example, the Source Routing setting is located in the `/proc/sys/net/ipv4/conf/all/accept_source_route` file. Simply display the contents of a file to see how the current running kernel is set up.

For each tunable kernel parameter shown, the change to the entry that needs to be affected can be modified or added to the `/etc/sysctl.conf` configuration file to make the change persistent after a reboots.

You can get a list of current kernel settings by using the command:

```
sysctl -a
```

It is even a very good idea to store the output of the kernel settings (for comparison or reference) by redirecting the output of the sysctl command to a file, for example

```
sysctl -A > /root/sysctl.settings.store
```

Because SUSE Linux Enterprise Server includes, by default, security-focused kernel tuning parameters, you will find the existing `/etc/sysctl.conf` file to be sparsely populated. You may choose to use the above mentioned "catalog" method of storing the complete gamut of kernel settings and then choose those parameters you want to be reset at reboot. You can place these in the `/etc/sysctl.conf` file where they will be picked up upon a reboot or they can be inserted immediately (into the running kernel) by running the command **sysctl** -p.

Many third-party applications like Oracle, SAP, DB2, Websphere, etc. recommend changing kernel parameters to ensure high performance for I/O or CPU processing. Having a full list of current settings can be helpful for reference.

### 3.9.1 Enable TCP SYN Cookie Protection (default in SUSE Linux Enterprise Server 12 SP1)

A SYN attack is a denial of service attack that consumes all the resources on a machine. Any server that is connected to a network is potentially subject to this attack. To enable TCP SYN Cookie Protection, edit the /etc/sysctl.conf file and ensure the following line and value exists:

```
net.ipv4.tcp_syncookies = 1
```

 Note

Despite the name of the configuration option, it applies to IP version 6 as well.

### 3.9.2 Disable IP Source Routing (default in SUSE Linux Enterprise Server 12 SP1)

Source Routing is used to specify a path or route through the network from source to destination. This feature can be used by network people for diagnosing problems. However, if an intruder was able to send a source routed packet into the network, then he could intercept the replies and your server might not know that it is not communicating with a trusted server.

```
net.ipv4.conf.all.accept_source_route = 0
```

or

```
net.ipv6.conf.all.accept_source_route = 0
```

### 3.9.3 Disable ICMP Redirect Acceptance

ICMP redirects are used by routers to tell the server that there is a better path to other networks than the one chosen by the server. However, an intruder could potentially use ICMP redirect packets to alter the host's routing table by causing traffic to use a path you did not intend. To disable ICMP Redirect Acceptance, edit the /etc/sysctl.conf file and add the following line:

```
net.ipv4.conf.all.accept_redirects = 0
```

or

```
net.ipv6.conf.all.accept_redirects = 0
```

### 3.9.4　Enable IP Spoofing Protection (default in SUSE Linux Enterprise Server 12 SP1)

IP spoofing is a technique where an intruder sends out packets which claim to be from another host by manipulating the source address. IP spoofing is very often used for denial of service attacks. For more information on IP Spoofing, see http://en.wikipedia.org/wiki/IP_address_spoofing

```
net.ipv4.conf.all.rp_filter = 1
```

### 3.9.5　Enable Ignoring to ICMP Requests

If you want or need Linux to ignore **ping** requests, edit the /etc/sysctl.conf file and add the following line:

```
net.ipv4.icmp_echo_ignore_all = 1
```

This cannot be done in many environments, as some monitoring systems use a rudimentary ICMP (ping) to determine the health of the device on the network (or at least its ability to respond).

### 3.9.6　Enable Ignoring Broadcasts Request (default in SUSE Linux Enterprise Server 12 SP1)

If you want or need Linux to ignore broadcast requests.

```
net.ipv4.icmp_echo_ignore_broadcasts = 1
```

### 3.9.7　Enable Bad Error Message Protection (default in SUSE Linux Enterprise Server 12 SP1)

To alert you about bad error messages in the network.

```
net.ipv4.icmp_ignore_bogus_error_responses = 1
```

## 3.9.8   Enable Logging of Spoofed Packets, Source Routed Packets, Redirect Packets

To turn on logging for Spoofed Packets, Source Routed Packets, and Redirect Packets, edit the /etc/sysctl.conf file and add the following line:

```
net.ipv4.conf.all.log_martians = 1
```

 Note

> Because of the way SUSE Linux Enterprise Server is set up (with rsyslog) for network event tracking, keep in mind that this can cause a large amount of messages to be logged.

## 3.9.9   Virtual Address Space Randomization

Starting with the 2.6.x kernel releases, Linux uses the address-space randomization technique to mitigate buffer overflows. For more information, see:

- http://searchenterpriselinux.techtarget.com/tip/Linux-virtual-address-randomization-and-impacting-buffer-overflows

- https://en.wikipedia.org/wiki/Address_space_layout_randomization

Since version 12, SUSE Linux Enterprise Server already comes with some buffer overflow mitigation techniques being enabled by default. One of them is Address Space Layout Randomization (ASLR).

ASLR should be enabled by default already. You can check the output of the following command (should be 2):

```
# cat /proc/sys/kernel/randomize_va_space
2
```

This randomizes the heap, stack, and load addresses of dynamically linked libraries. Programs that run privileged or process network data are already built using special compiler flags (PIE and _FORTIFY_SOURCE) to take even more advantage of randomizing the text and data segments as well.

Another protection is called No-Execute (NX) or Data Execution Prevention (DEP) which is enabled by default on the SUSE Linux Enterprise Server kernel for the x86 and x86_64 architecture.

Furthermore, since version 12, SUSE Linux Enterprise Server prevents leaking of internal kernel addresses to make kernel exploits harder by setting the `kptr_restrict`:

```
# cat /proc/sys/kernel/kptr_restrict
  1
```

On CPU's that support it (newer x86_64 CPUs) the kernel also uses the SMEP protection by default that prevents direct execution of userland code from inside the kernel. This is often used by kernel exploits and therefore a good hardening measure.

## 3.9.10  File system hardening

To mitigate vulnerabilities based on insecure file system access by privileged programs (tmp-races, TOCTOU) the Linux kernel offers two **sysctl** variables which should already be enabled by default on SUSE Linux Enterprise Server 12 SP1: `fs.protected_hardlinks` and `fs.protected_symlinks` or their corresponding `/proc` entries:

```
$ cat /proc/sys/fs/protected_hardlinks
1
$ cat /proc/sys/fs/protected_symlinks
1
```

By setting these variables, users can no longer create soft or hard links to files which they do not own. This mitigates a commonly used exploitation vector for programs which call open(2), creat(2) or similar functions without care.

### 3.9.11   Increased **dmesg** Restrictions

`dmesg` provides all kinds of system internal information, such as kernel addresses, crashes of services, and similar things that could be used by local attackers. This is why the access to **dmesg** is restricted to `root` by default. The behavior is controlled by the `kernel.dmesg_restrict` option (defaults to 1). If set to 0, any user can view the output of **dmesg**.

### 3.9.12   Filter access to /dev/mem (default in SUSE Linux Enterprise Server 12)

`/dev/mem` hosts an image of the system's main memory, including kernel and userspace memory. Allowing unfiltered access to this information is dangerous and therefore the Kernel on SUSE Linux Enterprise Server has been compiled with `CONFIG_STRICT_DEVMEM` enabled. This setting restricts userspace access to `/dev/mem` to memory mapped peripherals.

## 3.10   AppArmor

Included with SUSE Linux Enterprise Server, AppArmor is an application security tool designed to provide an easy-to-use security framework for your applications. AppArmor proactively protects the operating system and applications from external or internal threats, even zero-day attacks, by enforcing good behavior and preventing some unknown application flaws from being exploited. AppArmor security policies, called "profiles", completely define what system resources individual applications can access, and with what privileges. Several default profiles are included with AppArmor, and using a combination of advanced static analysis and learning-based tools, AppArmor profiles for even very complex applications can be deployed successfully in a matter of hours.

AppArmor consists of:

- A kernel extension which enforces the security profiles.

- A collection of RPMs, also shipped with SUSE Linux Enterprise Server that provides:

    - A set of AppArmor profiles for numerous programs that ship with SUSE Linux Enterprise Server

    - Tools to create and manage new and existing AppArmor profiles

- A YaST user interface to manage reports and notification of security events

- Documentation about the AppArmor tools

It is best to reboot a system after completing installation, so that AppArmor can confine all system daemons.

The AppArmor quick-start and administrative guides are available online here:

http://www.suse.com/documentation/apparmor/

For additional details and step-by-step instructions on the usage and configuration of AppArmor you can also refer to *Book "Security Guide"*.

## 3.11 SELinux

SELinux is an advanced technology for securing Linux systems. It is included with "basic enablement" in SUSE Linux Enterprise Server 12 SP1, and is included with some other distributions by default. Hardening Linux using SELinux technology, on its own, warrants its own security HOWTO and is out of scope for this guide. The book SELinux: NSA's Open Source Security Enhanced Linux [http://shop.oreilly.com/product/9780596007164.do] contains a very good description of its setup and usage. As part of the "basic enablement", SELinux will not be officially supported, but packages have now been added to SUSE Linux Enterprise Server 12 SP1 to enable its usage with minimal effort. While AppArmor is much easier to use and has a similar feature set, knowing both will most certainly be beneficial.

## 3.12 FTP, `telnet`, and `rlogin` (rsh)

The programs/protocols of FTP, `telnet`, and `rlogin` (`rsh`) are vulnerable to eavesdropping, which is one of the main reasons secure alternatives such as `ssh`, `scp` or `sftp` should be used instead. It is highly recommended not to run the insecure services. Because of the high risk, this guide does not cover these services (other than vsftp). It would also be a good idea (and part of our guidance, see next section) not to have FTP and Telnet server RPMs installed on the system. Note that the EAL 4+ evaluation had vsftp installed. The "vs" stands for "very secure"—which is a differentiator here when compared to normal FTP.

# 3.13   Removing Unnecessary Software Packages (RPMs)

A very important step in securing a Linux system is to determine the primary function(s) or role(s) of the Linux server. Otherwise, it can be difficult to understand what needs to be secured and securing these Linux systems can prove ineffective. Therefore, it is critical to look at the default list of software packages and remove any unnecessary packages or packages that do not comply with your defined security policies.

Doing this will result in fewer packages that require updates and will simplify maintenance efforts when security alerts and patches are released. It is a best practice not to install, among others, development packages or desktop software packages (for example, an X Server) on production servers. If you do not need them, you should also uninstall, for example, the Apache Web server or Samba file sharing server.

## ! Important: Requirements of Third-party Installers

Many third-party vendors like Oracle and IBM require a desktop environment and development libraries to run installers. To avoid this from having an impact on the security of their production servers, many organizations work around this by creating a silent installation (response file) in a development lab.

Also, other packages like FTP and Telnet daemons should not be installed as well unless there is a justified business reason for it (again, `ssh`, `scp` or `sftp` should be used as replacements).

One of the first action items should be to create a Linux image that *only* contains RPMs needed by the system and applications, and those needed for maintenance and troubleshooting purposes. A good approach is to start with a minimum list of RPMs and then add packages as needed. This process is time-consuming but usually worth the effort.

## ⚙ Tip: Just Enough Operating System (JeOS)

The SUSE Appliance Program includes a component called JeOS (Just Enough Operating System). JeOS has a very small footprint and can be customized to fit the specific needs of a system developer. Main uses of JeOS are for hardware/software appliance or virtual machine development. Key benefits of JeOS are efficiency, higher performance, increased security and simplified management.

If JeOS is not an option for you, a good choice is the minimal installation pattern.

To generate a list of all installed RPMs—use the following command:

```
rpm -qa
```

To retrieve details about a particular RPM (from the RPM itself), run:

```
rpm -qi package_name
```

To check for and report potential conflicts and dependencies when deleting an RPM, run:

```
rpm -e --test package_name
```

This can be very useful, as running the removal command without a test can often yield a mass of complaints and require manual recursive dependency hunting.

## 3.14  Patching Linux Systems

Building an infrastructure for patch management is another very important part of a proactive and secure production Linux environment.

It is recommended to have a written security policy and procedure to handle Linux security updates and issues. For example, a security policy should detail the time frame for assessment, testing, and roll out of patches. Network related security vulnerabilities should get the highest priority and should be addressed immediately within a short time frame. The assessment phase should occur within a testing lab, and initial roll out should occur on development systems first

A separate security log file should contain details on which Linux security announcements have been received, which patches have been researched and assessed, when patches have been applied, etc.

SUSE releases their patches in three categories, security, recommended and optional. There are a few options that can be used to keep systems patched, up to date and secure. Each system can register and then retrieve updates via the SUSE Update Web site using the included YaST tool—YaST Online Update. SUSE has also created the Subscription Management Tool (SMT), an efficient way to maintain a local repository of available/released patches/updates/fixes that systems can then pull from (reducing Internet traffic). SUSE also offers SUSE Manager for the maintenance, patching, reporting and centralized management of Linux systems, not only SUSE, but other distributions as well.

## 3.14.1  YaST Online Update

On a per-server basis, installation of important updates and improvements is possible using the YaST Online Update tool. Current updates for the SUSE Linux Enterprise family are available from the product specific update catalogs containing patches. Installation of updates and improvements is accomplished using YaST and selecting *Online Update* in the *Software* Group. All new patches (except the optional ones) that are currently available for your system will already be marked for installation. Clicking *Accept* will then automatically install these patches.

## 3.14.2  Automatic Online Update

YaST also offers the possibility to set up an automatic update. Select *Software › Automatic Online Update*. Configure a Daily or a Weekly update. Some patches, such as kernel updates, require user interaction, which would cause the automatic update procedure to stop. Check *Skip Interactive Patches* for the update procedure to proceed automatically.

In this case, run a manual Online Update from time to install patches that require interaction.

When *Only Download Patches* is checked, the patches are downloaded at the specified time but not installed. They must be installed manually using `rpm` or `zypper`.

## 3.14.3  Subscription Management Tool—SMT

The Subscription Management Tool for SUSE Linux Enterprise goes one step further than the Online Update process by establishing a proxy system with repository and registration targets. This helps customers centrally manage software updates within the firewall on a per-system basis, while maintaining their corporate security policies and regulatory compliance.

The downloadable SMT (http://download.suse.com/) is integrated with SUSE Customer Center (https://scc.suse.com/) and provides a repository and registration target that is synchronized with it. This can be very helpful in tracking entitlements in large deployments. The SMT maintains all the capabilities of SUSE Customer Center, while allowing a more secure centralized deployment. It is included with every SUSE Linux Enterprise subscription and is therefore fully supported.

The SMT provides an alternative to the default configuration, which requires opening the firewall to outbound connections for each device to receive updates. That requirement often violates corporate security policies and can be seen as a threat to regulatory compliance by some organizations. Through its integration with SUSE Customer Center, the SMT ensures that each device can receive its appropriate updates without the need to open the firewall, and without any redundant bandwidth requirements.

The SMT also enables customers to locally track their SUSE Linux Enterprise devices (that is servers, desktops, or Point of Service terminals) throughout their enterprise. Now they can easily determine how many entitlements are in need of renewal at the end of a billing cycle without having to physically walk through the data center to manually update spreadsheets.

The SMT informs the SUSE Linux Enterprise devices of any available software updates. Each device then obtains the required software updates from the SMT. The introduction of the SMT improves the interaction among SUSE Linux Enterprise devices within the network and simplifies how they receive their system updates. The SMT enables an infrastructure for several hundred SUSE Linux Enterprise devices per instance of each installation (depending on the specific usage profile). This offers more accurate and efficient server tracking.

In a nutshell, the Subscription Management Tool for SUSE Linux Enterprise provides customers with:

- Assurance of firewall and regulatory compliance

- Reduced bandwidth usage during software updates

- Full support under active subscription from SUSE

- Maintenance of existing customer interface with SUSE Customer Center

- Accurate server entitlement tracking and effective measurement of subscription usage

- Automated process to easily tally entitlement totals (no more spreadsheets!)

- Simple installation process that automatically synchronizes server entitlement with SUSE Customer Center

### 3.14.4   SUSE Manager

SUSE Manager automates Linux server management, allowing you to provision and maintain your servers faster and more accurately. It monitors the health of each Linux server from a single console so you can identify server performance issues before they impact your business. And it lets you comprehensively manage your Linux servers across physical, virtual and cloud environments while improving data center efficiency. SUSE Manager delivers complete life cycle management for Linux:

- Asset management

- Provisioning

- Package management

- Patch management

- Configuration management

- Redeployment

For more information on SUSE Manager refer to https://www.suse.com/products/suse-manager/.

## 3.15   Securing the Network—Open Network Ports Detection

Securing a server requires that you know what it is serving; what services are running. Default server installations may have services running that aren't self apparent and open network ports that they are using. So, one of the most important tasks is to detect and close network ports that are not needed. To get a list of listening network ports (TCP and UDP sockets), you can use the **netstat** service run the following command:

```
netstat -tulp
```

Be aware that **netstat** output can be wider than a default terminal screen. If the screen is too narrow, the options described above will likely cause the output to wrap and be less legible. Below is an example of output from the above command:

```
Proto Recv-Q Send-Q Local          Foreign        State   PID/Program
```

```
             Address          Address                    name
tcp  0    0    *:auth           *.*            LISTEN  2328/xinetd

tcp  0    0    local[...].:smtp *.*            LISTEN  2360/sendmail:acce

tcp  0    0    *:ssh            *.*            LISTEN  2317/sshd
```

From the output above you can see that three tcp-based services are running and listening: xinetd, sendmail, and sshd. Sendmail should not be configured to listen for incoming network connections unless the server running it is a designated as a mail or relay server. Running a port scan from another server can confirm that, but make sure to obtain proper permissions to scan/probe a machine on a production network.

 Important

> Some organizations consider port scans without permission a security offense.

Using the nmap tool, such a probe/scan can be run:

```
root #  nmap -sTU remote_host
Starting nmap 3.70 ( http://www.insecure.org/nmap/ ) at 2004-12-10 22:51 CST
Interesting ports on venus (192.168.2.101):
(The 3131 ports scanned but not shown below are in state: closed)
PORT      STATE        SERVICE
22/tcp    open         ssh
113/tcp   open         auth


Nmap run completed -- 1 IP address (1 host up) scanned in 221.669 seconds
```

Note that running the **nmap** command can take quite a while (in this example almost 4 minutes) depending on the options used. If you remove the UDP port scan (leave out the -U option), then **nmap** will finish the port scan nearly immediately. The results of **nmap** can vary widely and might not show all listening network sockets depending on the status of the SuSEFirewall2 (or other) and if it has been set up to block any ports.

From the sample run above, you see that the xinetd daemon is listening on port auth (port 113) for IDENT (for more information on this service, see *Section 3.16, "xinetd Services - Disabling"*). You can also see that sendmail is not listening for remote incoming network connections.

Another method to list all of the TCP and UDP sockets to which programs are listening (on a host) is to use the **lsof** command – which lists open files :

```
root #  lsof -i -n | egrep 'COMMAND|LISTEN|UDP'
COMMAND  PID   USER  FD   TYPE   DEVICE SIZE/OFF NODE NAME
sshd     2317  root  3u   IPv6   6579   0t0      TCP *:ssh (LISTEN)
xinetd   2328  root  5u   IPv4   6698   0t0      TCP *:auth (LISTEN)
sendmail 2360  root  3u   IPv4   6729   0t0      TCP 127.0.0.1:smtp (LISTEN)
```

# 3.16  xinetd Services - Disabling

The xinetd daemon is a replacement for inetd, the Internet services daemon. It monitors the ports for all network services configured in /etc/xinetd.d, and starts the services in response to incoming connections. To check if xinetd is enabled and running, execute:

```
root #  systemctl status xinetd
```

To check the current status of the xinetd service, execute:

```
root # systemctl status xinetd
```

If xinetd is active, it is very important to see which services are active and being controlled by xinetd. The following command will list all services configured in /etc/xinetd.d and whether xinetd monitors the ports for these services:

```
root #  chkconfig -list | awk '/xinetd based services/,/""/'
xinetd based services:

  chargen:      off
  chargen-udp:  off
  cups-lpd:     off
  cvs:          off
  daytime:      off
  daytime-udp:  off
  discard:      off
  discard-udp:  off
```

```
echo:          off

echo-udp:      off

netstat:       off

rsync:         off

sane-port:     off

servers:       off

services:      off

svnserve:      off

swat:          off

systat:        off

tftp:          on

time:          off

time-udp:      off

vnc:           off
```

To get a list of only active services for which xinetd monitors the ports, you could run (where the `-v` option of grep does an inverse-match) :

```
root #  chkconfig --list | awk '/xinetd based services/,/""/' | grep -v off
xinetd based services:


  tftp:          on
```

In the above example you can see that the `telnet-server` package is not installed on the system. If the Telnet Server package `telnet-server` would be installed, it would show up on the list whether it is active. Here is an example how to disable a service. Assuming the `tftp` service is active, run the following commands to disable it and to see how the telnet service entries are being updated:

```
# sudo systemctl status tftp
tftp.service - Tftp Server
Loaded: loaded (/usr/lib/systemd/system/tftp.service; static)
Active: active (running) since Fri 2014-09-05 07:56:23 CEST; 2h 1min ago

# sudo cat /etc/xinetd.d/tftp | grep disable
   disable = no
```

```
# sudo systemctl disable tftp


# systemctl status tftp
tftp.service - Tftp Server
Loaded: loaded (/usr/lib/systemd/system/tftp.service; static)
Active: inactive (dead)


# sudo cat /etc/xinetd.d/tftp | grep disable
        disable = yes
```

For the TFTP service it would be better to remove the package from the system since removal is always safer than disabling (when possible):

```
rpm -e tftp
```

## 3.16.1   Inventory xinetd services

It is important to investigate *all* active xinetd services and to disable them (or remove their packages) if they are not needed. To find out what a service does, here is a viable approach. Using the tftp service as an example and assuming its function is unknown and it is listed as an active service. Execute the following commands:

```
root #  grep " server" /etc/xinetd.d/tftp
  server = /usr/sbin/in.tftpd
  server_args = -s /tftpboot
```

To read the manual:

```
root #  man in.tftpd
TFTPD(8)                  System Manager's Manual                  TFTPD(8)




NAME
        tftpd - IPv4 Trivial File Transfer Protocol server
```

```
SYNOPSIS

     in.tftpd [options...]  directory...


DESCRIPTION

     tftpd  is  a  server  for the Trivial File Transfer Protocol.
     The TFTP protocol is extensively used to support remote boot-
     ing  of  diskless devices.  The server is normally started by
     inetd, but can also run stand-alone.
[...]
```

To determine what package supplies the in.tftpd binary:

```
root #  rpm -qf /usr/sbin/in.tftpd
tftp-0.48-101.16
```

To get a description of TFTP and its usage, etc:

```
root #  rpm -qi tftp-0.48-101.16| awk '/Description/,/""/'
Description :
The Trivial File Transfer Protocol (TFTP) is normally used only for
booting diskless workstations and for getting or saving network
component configuration files.
```

To get a list of what files are installed via the TFTP package (RPM), execute the **rpm** command with the following options:

```
root #  rpm -ql tftp-0.48-101.16
/etc/xinetd.d/tftp
/usr/bin/tftp
/usr/sbin/in.tftpd
/usr/share/doc/packages/tftp
/usr/share/doc/packages/tftp/README
/usr/share/doc/packages/tftp/README.security
/usr/share/doc/packages/tftp/sample.rules
/usr/share/man/man1/tftp.1.gz
/usr/share/man/man8/in.tftpd.8.gz
/usr/share/man/man8/tftpd.8.gz
```

This example described what could be done to find out information about services (specifically ones started by `xinetd`) even if an online manual did not exist for the binary `in.ftpd`. This example yielded a man page – but you may not always find one. The RPM commands in the example are very commonly used for a variety of reasons. It is also possible to use the YaST software management interface to retrieve all of the resultant information – however having a knowledge of RPM command syntax can save quite a bit of time. Again to disable the TFTP service, execute the following command:

```
root # systemctl disable tftp
```

The `xinetd` daemon is quite flexible and has many features. Here are a few functionalities of `xinetd`:

- Access control for TCP, UDP, and RPC services.

- Access limitations based on time.

- Provides mechanisms to prevent DoS attacks.

For more specific information on Xinetd, review the documentation and usage examples at the xinetd Web site http://www.xinetd.org/.

## 3.17  Securing Postfix

Postfix is a replacement for Sendmail and has several security advantages over Sendmail. Postfix is the default mail system in SUSE Linux Enterprise Server and consists of several small programs that each perform their own small task—most of these programs run in a chroot jail. This is one of the reasons Postfix is recommended over Sendmail.

Linux servers that are not dedicated mail or relay servers should not accept external e-mails. However, it is important for production servers to send local e-mails to a relay server—some security setups (for example the seccheck scripts) can be configured to send e-mails to someone other than `root`, even off the local system.

Verify the following parameters in `/etc/postfix/main.cf` are set to ensure that Postfix accepts only local e-mails for delivery (look towards the bottom of the file as the top portion is mostly commented-out example entries and explanations):

```
mydestination = $myhostname, localhost.$mydomain, localhost
```

```
inet_interfaces = localhost
```

The `mydestination` parameter lists all domains to receive e-mails for. The `inet_interfaces` parameter specifies the network to listen on. After reconfiguring Postfix, a restart of the mail system is necessary:

```
root # systemctl restart postfix
```

Verify that Postfix is not listening for network requests (incoming) by running one of these commands from another host:

```
nmap -sT -p 25 remote_host
telnet <remote_host> 25
```

 Note

Running these commands on the local host will provide inaccurate results since Postfix is supposed to accept connections from the local node – use an external host for correct results.

## 3.18 File Systems: Securing NFS

NFS (Network File System) allows servers to share files over a network. But like all network services using NFS involves risks.

Here are some basic rules:

- NFS should not be enabled if not needed.

- If NFS is truly needed, use a TCP wrapper to restrict remote access.

- Ensure to export only to those hosts that really need access.

- Use a fully qualified domain name to diminish any spoofing attempts.

- Export only as read-only whenever possible.

- Use NFS only over TCP.

If you do not have shared directories to export, then ensure that the NFS service is *not* enabled nor running on the system:

Check the nfs service status:

```
root #  systemctl status nfsserver
```

Check the current targets:

```
root #   ls /etc/systemd/system/*.wants/nfsserver.service
```

## 3.18.1   Enabling and Starting NFS Server

If NFS must be used, it can be activated using the following commands on SUSE Linux Enterprise Server or more simply and securely with the YaST plug-in (ncurses). Access it directly from command line with **yast nfs_server** or **yast nfs_client** – or manually:

```
root # systemctl enable nfs
systemctl start nfs
```

Portmapper information:

```
root #   rpcinfo -p server
   program vers proto    port
    100000   2   tcp     111  portmapper
    100000   2   udp     111  portmapper
    100003   2   udp    2049  nfs
    100003   3   udp    2049  nfs
    100003   2   tcp    2049  nfs
    100003   3   tcp    2049  nfs
    100005   1   udp     623  mountd
    100005   1   tcp     626  mountd
    100005   2   udp     623  mountd
    100005   2   tcp     626  mountd
    100005   3   udp     623  mountd
    100005   3   tcp     626  mountd
```

If you run it from an "untrusted" server or network, you should get the following output:

```
root #  rpcinfo -p server
No remote programs registered.
```

## 3.18.2  Exporting NFS

To allow a client access to a file system or directory, the /etc/exports file serves as the access control list. To give the network "network.example.com" read-only access to /pub, the entries in /etc/exports would look like as follows:

```
    /pub *.network.example.com(ro,sync)
```

It is very important *not* to give write access to NFS clients if not absolutely needed! Entries in /etc/exports are exported read-only ( ro option) by default. To allow servers sles-ha1, sles-ha2 and sles-ha3 read-write access to the /data/MYSQL directory, the entries in / etc/exports would look like as follows:

```
/data/MYSQL sles-ha1.example.com(rw,sync) sles-ha2.example.com(rw,sync) sles-
ha3.example.com(rw,sync)
```

Note that the options *must not* be separated from the host names or networks with whitespace(s). Also, fully qualified domain names should *always* be used to diminish spoofing attempts. All entries in /etc/exports are exported with the root_squash option ("root squashing") by default. This means that a root user on a client machine does not have root privileges (root access) to files on exported NFS. It is not recommended to turn "root squashing" off using the no_root_squash option! After you have made all your entries in /etc/exports, you can export all file systems/directories using the following command:

```
exportfs -a
```

To unexport all shared file systems/directories, run:

```
exportfs -ua
```

To see all shared file systems/directories, run:

```
root #  showmount -e localhost
Export list for localhost:


/pub *.network.example.com/data/MYSQL
sles-ha1.example.com,sles-ha2.example.com,sles-ha3.example.com
```

### 3.18.3   Using NFS over TCP

If you need NFS, it is recommended to use NFS only over TCP since NFS over UDP is not secure. All 2.4 and later kernels support NFS over TCP on the client side. Server support for TCP appeared in later 2.4 kernels and beyond. To mount a shared directory using NFS over TCP, it is necessary to use the `proto=tcp` mount option:

```
mount -o proto=tcp server_name:/pub /usr/local/pub
```

Verify that the target directory, in this case `/usr/local/pub`, exists on the client:

```
root #  mount [...] server_name:/pub on
/usr/local/pub type nfs (rw,proto=tcp,addr=192.168.1.110)
```

To have the shared directory mounted on the client at boot time, use the `/etc/fstab` file. For the above example, the `/etc/fstab` entry could look like this:

```
server_name:/pub /usr/local/pub nfs rsize=8192,wsize=8192,timeo=14,intr,tcp 0 0
```

## 3.19   Copying Files Using SSH Without Providing Login Prompts

This example is needed in some cases to enable files to be copied over the network using SSH without providing an interactive login prompt. This allows trusted hosts to be set up—an example of federation.

SSH can allow a forced command using the "command" option. Using this option it is possible to disable scp (secure copy) and enforce every passed **ssh** command to be ignored. On the server side where you want to retrieve the file from, add the following entry to the beginning of the SSH key in the ~/.ssh/authorized_keys2 file (the ~ represents a particular users home directory – root's home directory is /root – other users typically reside in /home/*username*):

```
command="/bin/cat ~/<file_name>" ssh-dss XXXYYYzzZ1122AAbbCC...{etc}
```

To copy now the file from the remote server, run the following command:

ssh *user* @ *server*  *local_file*

Since **/bin/cat** is run on the server side, its output needs to be redirected to the local file.

Another approach is to replace the **/bin/cat** (referenced above) with your own script that checks the passed SSH commands by reading the environment variable $SSH_ORIGINAL_COMMAND. For example:

```
#!/bin/ksh
 if [[ $SSH_ORIGINAL_COMMAND = "File1" ||
      $SSH_ORIGINAL_COMMAND = "File2" ]]
 then
     /bin/cat $SSH_ORIGINAL_COMMAND
 else
     echo "Invalid file name!"
     exit 1
 fi
```

So you replace the **/bin/cat** portion with the script name in ~/.ssh/authorized_keys2, and run the following command to copy Foo1:

```
ssh user@server Foo1 > local_file
```

To copy Foo 2, run:

```
ssh user@server Foo2 > local_file
```

With the modifications above, every other variety of passed parameters will return errors.

## 3.20 Checking File Permissions and Ownership

The following sections deal with some ways the default permissions and file settings can be modified to enhance the security of a host. It is important to note that the use of the default SUSE Linux Enterprise Server utilities like **seccheck** - can be run to lock down and improve the general file security and user environment. However, it is beneficial to understand how to modify these things.

SUSE Linux Enterprise Server hosts include 3 defaults settings for file permissions: `permissions.easy`, `permissions.secure`, and `permissions.paranoid`, all located in the `/etc` directory. The purpose of these files is to define special permissions, such as world-writable directories or, for files, the setuser ID bit (programs with the setuser ID bit set do not run with the permissions of the user that has launched it, but with the permissions of the file owner, usually `root`).

Administrators can use the file `/etc/permissions.local` to add their own settings. The easiest way to implement one of the default permission rule-sets above is to use the *Local Security* module in YaST.

Each of the following topics will be modified by a selected rule-set, but the information is important to understand on its own.

## 3.21 Default umask

The **umask** (user file-creation mode mask) command is a shell built-in command which determines the default file permissions for newly created files. This can be overwritten by system calls but many programs and utilities use **umask**. By default, SUSE sets **umask** to 022. You can modify this by changing the value in `/etc/profile`.

The **id** command will print out the current user identity information. Example from a non-root prompt:

```
tux > id
uid=1000(ne0) gid=100(users) groups=16(dialout),33(video),100(users)
```

And to determine the active umask – use the umask command:

```
tux > umask
0022
```

Now, for comparison sake, the same commands from the root user:

```
root #  id
uid=0(root) gid=0(root) groups=0(root)
root #  umask
0022
```

## 3.22 SUID/SGID Files

When the SUID (set user ID) or SGID (set group ID) bits are set on an executable, it executes with the UID or GID of the owner of the executable rather than that of the person executing it. This means that, for example, all executables that have the SUID bit set and are owned by root are executed with the UID of root. A good example is the passwd command that allows ordinary users to update the password field in the /etc/shadow file which is owned by root.

But SUID/SGID bits can be misused when the SUID/SGID executable has a security hole. Therefore, you should search the entire system for SUID/SGID executables and document it. For example, ensure that code developers do not set SUID/SGID bits on their programs if it is not an absolute requirement. Very often you can use workarounds like removing the executable bit for world/others. However, a better approach is to change the design of the software if possible.

To search the entire system for SUID or SGID files, you can run the following command:

```
find / -path /proc -prune -o -type f -perm '/6000' -ls
```

The -prune option in this example is used to skip the /proc file system.

## 3.23 World-Writable Files

World-writable files are a security risk since it allows anyone to modify them. Additionally, world-writable directories allow anyone to add or delete files. To locate world-writable files and directories, you can use the following command:

```
find / -path /proc -prune -o -perm -2 ! -type l -ls
```

The `! -type l` parameter skips all symbolic links since symbolic links are always world-writable. However, this is not a problem as long as the target of the link is not world-writable, which is checked by the above find command.

World-writable directories with sticky bit—directory or file ownership where only the item's owner, the directory's owner, or `root` can rename or delete files—such as the `/tmp` directory do not allow anyone except the owner of a file to delete or modify it in this directory. The sticky bit makes files stick to the user who created it and it prevents other users from deleting and renaming the files. Therefore, depending on the purpose of the directory world-writable directories with sticky are usually not an issue. An example is the `/tmp` directory:

```
tux > ls -ld /tmp
drwxrwxrwt 18 root root 16384 Dec 23 22:20 /tmp
```

The `t` mode, which denotes the sticky bit, allows files to be deleted and renamed only if the user is the owner of this file or the owner of the directory.

SUSE Linux Enterprise Server supports file capabilities to allow more fine grained privileges to be given to programs rather than the full power of root:

```
# getcap -v /usr/bin/ping
      /usr/bin/ping = cap_new_raw+eip
```

The previous command only grants the CAP_NET_RAW capability to whoever executes ping. In case of vulnerabilities inside ping, an attacker can gain at most this capability in contrast to full root when granting the ping binary suid root rights. Whenever possible, file capabilities should be chosen in favor of the suid-to-root bit. But this only applies when the binary is suid to root, not to other users such as `news`, `lp` and alike.

# 3.24  Orphaned or Unowned Files

Files not owned by any user or group might not necessarily be a security problem in itself. However, unowned files could pose a security problem in the future. For example, if a new user is created and the new users happens to get the same UID as the unowned files have, then this new user will automatically become the owner of these files.

To locate files not owned by any user or group, use the following command:

```
find / -path /proc -prune -o -nouser -o -nogroup
```

## 3.25  Restricting Access to Removable Media

In some environments it is required to restrict access to removable media such as USB storage or optical devices. The tools coming with the `udisks2` package help with such a configuration.

1. Create a rules file `/etc/polkit-1/rules.d/01-restrict-removable-media.rules` similar to the following:

```
// Allow users in group 'mmedia_all' to mount/unmount all type of drives
// Allow users in group 'mmedia_removable' to mount/umount USB storage drives
// Allow users in group 'mmedia_optical' to mount/unmount Optical drives
polkit.addRule(function(action, subject) {
  if (/^org\.freedesktop\.udisks2\.filesystem-.*mount.*$/.test(action.id) &&
  action.lookup("drive.removable") == "true") {
    if (subject.isInGroup("mmedia_all")) {
      return polkit.Result.YES;
    } else {
      if (/.*optical.*/.test(action.lookup("drive.removable.media"))) {
        if (subject.isInGroup("mmedia_optical"))
        return polkit.Result.YES;
      } else if (/.*floppy.*/.test(action.lookup("drive.removable.media"))) {
        return polkit.Result.NO;
      } else if (action.lookup("drive.removable.bus") == "usb") {
        if (subject.isInGroup("mmedia_removable"))
        return polkit.Result.YES;
      }
      return polkit.Result.NO;
    }
  }
});
```

 **Important:** Naming of the Rules File

Rules files are processed in alphabetical order. Functions are called in the order they were added until one of the functions returns a value. Hence, to add an authorization rule that is processed before other rules, put it in a file in /etc/polkit-1/rules.d with a name that sorts before other rules files, for example `01-restrict-remov-able-media.rules`. Each function should return a value from `polkit.Result`.

2. Restart `udisks2`:

```
systemctl restart udisks2
```

3. Restart `polkit`

```
systemctl restart polkit
```

4. In YaST, click *Security and Users* › *User and Group Management* › *Groups* to create the three groups `mmedia_all`, `mmedia_optical`, and `mmedia_removable`. Then add the users to these groups as wanted.

## 3.26 Various Account Checks

### 3.26.1 Unlocked Accounts

It is important that all system and vendor accounts that are not used for logins are locked. To get a list of unlocked accounts on your system, you can check for accounts that do *not* have an encrypted password string starting with ! or * in the /etc/shadow file. If you lock an account using **passwd** -l, it will put a !! in front of the encrypted password, effectively disabling the password. If you lock an account using **usermod** -L, it will put a ! in front of the encrypted password. Many system and shared accounts are usually locked by default by having a `*` or `!!` in the password field which renders the encrypted password into an invalid string. Hence, to get a list of all unlocked (encryptable) accounts, run (**egrep** is used to allow use of regular-expressions):

```
egrep -v ':\*|:\!' /etc/shadow | awk -F: '{print $1}'
```

Also make sure all accounts have a `x` in the password field in `/etc/passwd`. The following command lists all accounts that do not have a `x` in the password field:

```
grep -v ':x:' /etc/passwd
```

An `x` in the password fields means that the password has been shadowed, for example the encrypted password needs to be looked up in the `/etc/shadow` file. If the password field in `/etc/passwd` is empty, then the system will not look up the shadow file and it will not prompt the user for a password at the login prompt.

## 3.26.2  Unused Accounts

All system or vendor accounts that are not being used by users, applications, by the system or by daemons should be removed from the system. You can use the following command to find out if there are any files owned by a specific account:

```
find / -path /proc -prune -o -user account -ls
```

The `-prune` option in this example is used to skip the /proc file system. If you are sure that an account can be deleted, you can remove the account using the following command:

```
userdel -r account
```

Without the `-r` option **userdel** will not delete the user's home directory and mail spool (`/var/spool/mail/user`). Note that many system accounts have no home directory.

## 3.27  Enabling Password Aging

Password expirations are a general best practice—but might need to be excluded for some system and shared accounts (for example Oracle, etc.). Expiring password on those accounts could lead to system outages if the application account expires.

Typically a corporate policy should be developed that dictates rules/procedures regarding password changes for system and shared accounts. However, normal user account passwords should expire automatically. The following example shows how password expiration can be set up for individual user accounts.

The following files and parameters in the table can be used when a new account is created with the **useradd** command. Settings such as these are stored for each user account in the /etc/shadow file. If using the YaST tool (*User and Group Management*) to add users, the settings are available on a per-user basis. Here are the various settings—some of which can also be system-wide (for example modification of /etc/login.defs and /etc/default/useradd):

| /etc/login.defs | PASS_MAX_DAYS | Maximum number of days a password is valid. |
|---|---|---|
| /etc/login.defs | PASS_MIN_DAYS | Minimum number of days before a user can change the password since the last change. |
| /etc/login.defs | PASS_WARN_AGE | Number of days when the password change reminder starts. |
| /etc/default/useradd | INACTIVE | Number of days after password expiration that account is disabled. |
| /etc/default/useradd | EXPIRE | Account expiration date in the format YYYY-MM-DD. |

 Note

Users created prior to these modifications will not be affected.

Ensure that the above parameters are changed in the /etc/login.defs and /etc/default/useradd files. Review of the /etc/shadow file will show how these settings get stored after adding a user.

To create a new user account, execute the following command:

```
useradd -c "Test User" -g users test
```

The `-g` option specifies the primary group for this account:

```
root #  id test
uid=509(test) gid=100(users) groups=100(users)
```

The settings in `/etc/login.defs` and `/etc/default/useradd` are recorded for the test user in the `/etc/shadow` file as follows:

```
root #  grep test /etc/shadow
test:!!:12742:7:60:7:14::
```

Password aging can be modified at any time by use of the **chage** command. To disable password aging for system and shared accounts, you can run the following **chage** command:

```
chage -M -1 system_account_name
```

To get password expiration information:

```
chage -l system_account_name
```

For example:

```
root #  chage -l test
Minimum: 7
Maximum: 60
Warning: 7
Inactive: 14
Last Change: Jan 11, 2015
Password Expires: Mar 12, 2015
Password Inactive: Mar 26, 2015
Account Expires: Never
```

# 3.28   Stronger Password Enforcement

On an audited system it is important to restrict people from using simple passwords that can be cracked too easily. Writing down complex passwords is all right as long as they are stored securely. Some will argue that strong passwords protect you against dictionary attacks and those type of attacks can be defeated by locking accounts after a few failed attempts. However, this is not always an option. If set up like this, locking system accounts could bring down your applications and systems which would be nothing short of a denial of service attack – another issue.

At any rate, it is important to practice effective password management safety. Most companies require that passwords have at the very least a number, one lowercase letter, and one uppercase letter. Policies vary, but maintaining a balance between password strength/complexity and management is sometimes difficult.

# 3.29   Leveraging an Effective PAM stack

Linux-PAM (Pluggable Authentication Modules for Linux) is a suite of shared libraries that enable the local system administrator to choose how applications authenticate users.

It is strongly recommended to familiarize oneself with the capabilities of PAM – and how this architecture can be leveraged to provide the best authentication setup for an environment. This configuration can be done once – and implemented across all systems (a standard) or can be enhanced for individual hosts (enhanced security – by host / service / application). The key is to realize how flexible the architecture is.

To learn more about the PAM architecture – you can find PAM documentation on a SUSE Linux Enterprise Server system in the `/usr/share/doc/packages/pam` directory (in a variety of formats).

The following discussions are examples of how to modify the default PAM stacks—specifically around password policies—for example password strength, password re-use and account locking. While these are only a few of the possibilities, they serve as a good start and demonstrate PAM's flexibility.

### 3.29.1 Password Strength

SUSE Linux Enterprise Server can leverage the `pam_cracklib` library to test for weak passwords – and to suggest using a stronger one if it determines obvious weakness. The following parameters represent an example that could be part of a corporate password policy or something required because of audit constraints.

The PAM libraries follow a defined flow. The best way to design the perfect stack usually is to consider all of the requirements and policies and draw out a flow chart.

TABLE 3.1: SAMPLE RULES/CONSTRAINTS FOR PASSWORD ENFORCEMENT

| | | |
|---|---|---|
| `pam_cracklib.so` | `minlen=8` | Minimum length of password is 8 |
| `pam_cracklib.so` | `lcredit=-1` | Minimum number of lower-case letters is 1 |
| `pam_cracklib.so` | `ucredit=-1` | Minimum number of upper-case letters is 1 |
| `pam_cracklib.so` | `dcredit=-1` | Minimum number of digits is 1 |
| `pam_cracklib.so` | `ocredit=-1` | Minimum number of other characters is 1 |

To set up these password restrictions, use the **pam-config** tool and specify the parameters you want to configure. For example, the minimum length parameter could be modified like this:

```
pam-config -a --cracklib-minlen=8 --cracklib-retry=3 \
--cracklib-lcredit=-1 --cracklib-ucredit=-1 --cracklib-dcredit=-1 \
--cracklib-ocredit=-1 --cracklib
```

Now verify that the new password restrictions work for new passwords. Simply login to a non-root account and change the password using the **passwd** command. Note that the above requirements are not enforced if you run the **passwd** command under root.

## 3.29.2  Restricting Use of Previous Passwords

The `pam_unix2` module parameter `remember` can be used to configure the number of previous passwords that cannot be reused. And the `pam_cracklib` module parameter `difok` can be used to specify the number of characters that must be different between the old and the new password.

The following example describes how to implement password restrictions on a system so that a password cannot be reused for at least 6 months and that at least 3 characters must be different between the old and new password.

Recall that in the section *Section 3.27, "Enabling Password Aging"* we set `PASS_MIN_DAYS` to `7`, which specifies the minimum number of days allowed between password changes. Therefore, if `pam_unix2` is configured to remember `26` passwords, then the previously used passwords cannot be reused for at least 6 months (26*7 days).

Here is an example of an enhanced pam stack. It is possible to edit the `/etc/pam.d/com-mon-auth` file to add/change modules used and how they react. Consider the following `pam_cracklib` and `pam_unix2` arguments—keeping in mind how the pam rules are processed:

```
auth        required      pam_env.so
auth        sufficient    pam_unix2.so likeauth nullok
auth        required      pam_deny.so
account     required      pam_unix2.so
account     sufficient    pam_succeed_if.so uid < 100 quiet
account     required      pam_permit.so
password    requisite     pam_cracklib.so retry=3 minlen=8 lcredit=-1
ucredit=-1 dcredit=-1 ocredit=-1 difok=3
password    sufficient    pam_unix2.so use_authtok sha512 shadow
                                  remember=26
password    required      pam_deny.so
session     required      pam_limits.so
session     required      pam_unix2.so
```

 Tip

You can configure and fine tune `pam_unix2.so` behavior in the `/etc/default/passwd` file.

### 3.29.3  Locking User Accounts After Too Many Login Failures

It is not generally recommend that a host automatically locks system and shared accounts after too many failed login or su attempts. This could lead to outages if the application's account gets locked because of too many login failures like in this example for an Oracle shared account:

```
root #  su oracle -c id
su: incorrect password
```

This could be an easy target for a denial of service attack. The following example shows how to lock only individual user accounts after too many failed su or login attempts. Add the following two lines to the /etc/pam.d/common-auth:

```
auth        required        pam_tally.so onerr=fail no_magic_root

[...]

auth        required        pam_tally.so per_user deny=5 no_magic_root reset
```

The first added line counts failed login and failed su attempts for each user. The default location for attempted accesses is recorded in /var/log/faillog.

The second added line specifies to lock accounts automatically after 5 failed login or su attempts (deny=5). The counter will be reset to 0 (reset) on successful entry if deny=$n$ was not exceeded. But you do not want system or shared accounts to be locked after too many login failures (denial of service attack).

It is also possible to add the lock_time=$n$ parameter, and then optionally the unlock_time=$n$ parameter. For example, setting the lock_time=60 would deny access for 60 seconds after a failed attempt. The unlock_time=$n$ option would then allow access after n seconds after an account has been locked. If this option is used the user will be locked out for the specified amount of time after he exceeded his maximum allowed attempts. Otherwise the account is locked until the lock is removed by a manual intervention of the system administrator. See the pam_tally man page for more information.

To exempt system and shared accounts from the deny=$n$ parameter, the per_user parameter was added to the module. The per_user parameter instructs the module *not* to use the deny=$n$ limit for accounts where the maximum number of login failures is set explicitly. For example:

```
root #  pam_tally2 -u oracle
    Login     Failures Latest failure                              From
```

```
    oracle    0       Fri Dec 10 23:57:55 -0600 2005 on unknown
```

To instruct the module to activate the deny=*n* limit for this account again, run:

```
pam_tally2 -u oracle deny=n
```

By default, the maximum number of login failures for each account is set to zero (0) which instructs pam_tally2 to leverage the deny=*n* parameter. To see failed login attempts, run:

```
pam_tally2
```

Make sure to test these changes (and *any* changes – for that matter) thoroughly on your system using **ssh** and **su**, and make sure the root id does not get locked! To lock/unlock accounts manually, you can run one of the following commands:

**Locking**

```
passwd -l user
        usermod -L user
```

**Unlocking**

```
passwd -u user
usermod -U user
```

# 3.30  Preventing Accidental Denial of Service

Linux allows you to set limits on the amount of system resources that users and groups can consume. This is also very handy if bugs in programs cause them to use up too much resources (for example memory leaks), slow down the machine, or even render the system unusable. Incorrect settings can allow programs to use too many resources which may make the server unresponsive to new connections or even local logins (for example if a program uses up all available file handles on the host). This can also be a security concern if someone is allowed to consume all system resources and therefore cause a denial of service attack – either unplanned or worse, planned. Setting resource limits for users and groups may be an effective way to protect systems, depending on the environment.

## 3.30.1  Example for Restricting System Resources

The following example demonstrates the practical usage of setting or restricting system resource consumption for an Oracle user account. For a list of system resource settings, see `/etc/security/limits.conf` or **`man limits.conf`**.

Most shells like Bash provide control over various resources (for example the maximum allowable number of open file descriptors or the maximum number of processes) that are available on a per/user basis. To examine all current limits in the shell execute:

```
ulimit -a
```

For more information on **`ulimit`** for the Bash shell, examine the Bash man pages.

 **Important:** Setting Limits for SSH Sessions

Setting "hard" and "soft" limits might not behave as expected when using an SSH session. To see valid behavior it may be necessary to login as root and then su to the id with limits (for example, `oracle` in these examples). Resource limits should also work assuming the application has been started automatically during the boot process. It may be necessary to set `UsePrivilegeSeparation` in `/etc/ssh/sshd_config` to "no" and restart the SSH daemon (**`systemctl restart sshd`**) if it seems that the changes to resource limits are not working (via SSH). However this is not generally recommended – as it weakens a systems security.

**Tip:** Disabling Password Logins via **`ssh`**

You can add some extra security to your server by disabling password authentication for SSH. Remember that you need to have SSH keys configured, otherwise you cannot access the server. To disable password login, add the following lines to `/etc/ssh/sshd_config`:

```
UseLogin no
UsePAM no
PasswordAuthentication no
PubkeyAuthentication yes
```

In this example, a change to the number of file handles or open files that the user `oracle` can use is made by editing `/etc/security/limits.conf` as `root` making the following changes:

```
oracle          soft    nofile      4096
oracle          hard    nofile      63536
```

The soft limit in the first line defines the limit on the number of file handles (open files) that the `oracle` user will have after login. If the user sees error messages about running out of file handles, then the user can increase the number of file handles like in this example up to the hard limit (in this example 63536) by executing:

```
ulimit -n 63536
```

You can set the soft and hard limits higher if necessary.

 Note

It is important to be judicious with the usage of ulimits. Allowing a "hard" limit for "nofile" for a user that equals the kernel limit (`/proc/sys/fs/file-max`) is very bad! If the user consumes all the available file handles, the system cannot initiate new logins as accessing (opening) PAM modules which are required for performing a login will not be possible.

You also need to ensure that `pam_limits` is either configured globally in `/etc/pam.d/common-auth`, or for individual services like SSH, su, login, and telnet in:

`/etc/pam.d/sshd` (for SSH)

`/etc/pam.d/su` (for su)

`/etc/pam.d/login` (local logins and telnet)

If you do not want to enable it for all logins, there is a specific PAM module that will read the `/etc/security/limits.conf` file. Entries in pam configuration directives will have entries like:

```
session     required      /lib/security/pam_limits.so
session     required      /lib/security/pam_unix.so
```

It is important to note that changes are not immediate and require a new login session:

```
root #  su — oracle
```

```
tux > ulimit -n
4096
```

Note that these examples are specific to the Bash shell - **ulimit** options are different for other shells. The default limit for the user `oracle` is `4096`. To increase the number of file handles the user `oracle` can use to `63536`, do:

```
root #  su – oracle
tux >  ulimit -n
4096
tux >  ulimit -n 63536
tux >  ulimit -n
63536
```

Making this permanent requires the addition of the setting, `ulimit -n 63536`, (again, for Bash) to the users profile (`~/.bashrc` or `~/.profile` file) which is the user start-up file for the Bash shell on SUSE Linux Enterprise Server (to verify your shell run: echo `$SHELL`). To do this you could simply type (or copy/paste – if you are reading this on the system) the following commands for the Bash shell of the user `oracle`:

```
root #  su - oracle
tux >  cat >> ~oracle/.bash_profile << EOF
ulimit -n 63536
EOF
```

## 3.31   Displaying Login Banners

It is often necessary to place a banner on login screens on all servers for legal/audit policy reasons and to deter intruders, etc.

If you want to print a legal banner after a user logs in using SSH, local console, etc., you can leverage the `/etc/motd` (motd = message of the day) file. The file exists on SUSE, however it is empty. Simply add content to the file that is applicable/required by the organization.

 Note: Banner Length

> Try to keep the content to a single page (or less), as it will scroll the screen if it does not fit.

For SSH you can edit the "Banner" parameter in the `/etc/ssh/sshd_config` file which will then appropriately display the banner text before the login prompt. For local console logins you can edit the `/etc/issue` file which will display the banner before the login prompt. For GDM, you could make the following changes to require a user to acknowledge the legal banner by selecting *Yes* or *No*. Edit the `/etc/gdm/PreSession/Default` file and add the following lines at the beginning of the script:

```
if ! gdialog --yesno '\nThis system is classified...\n' 10 10; then
    sleep 10
    exit 1;
fi
```

The `This system is classified...` test should be replaced with the valid text. It is important to note that this dialog will not prevent a login from progressing.

## 3.32 Miscellaneous

### 3.32.1 Host-Based Linux Monitoring and Intrusion Detection

Before you place a host into production or even on a network, consider the use of an system integrity checker, like **seccheck** (already discussed in *Section 3.4, "Verifying Security Action with seccheck"*, so in case of unauthorized changes, notifications will be issued. Also consider the use of an intrusion detection environment, like AIDE, the Advanced Intrusion Detection Environment.

AIDE is a GPL licensed and open source intrusion detection system. It could be considered a system fingerprinting mechanism. AIDE works by creating a database containing information about the files on your system. The database is created from rules laid out in the configuration file aide.conf. When AIDE is run, this database is referenced to check for changes (or created for the first time). Assuming a comparison check is being run, any changes not permitted by the configuration file are reported.

By leveraging AIDE—storing a copy of the host's database in a secure location—and comparing it (on a scheduled basis or as part of a forensic effort), system integrity/insurance can be a matter of heuristics and procedure. If an intruder compromises your system, the comparison effort will enable an administrator or security officer to know what has changed on the host. The initial database should be created as a final step—*before* a system gets deployed into production.

It is outside the scope of this article to cover Linux Monitoring and detailed Intrusion Detection systems (IDS) or solutions, however there is a plethora of information about configuring AIDE or other solutions and many informative articles on the Web.


## 3.32.2   Connect Accounting Utilities

Here is a list of commands you can use to get data about user logins:

`who`. Lists currently logged in users.

`w`. Shows who is logged in and what they are doing.

`last`. Shows a list of last logged in users, including login time, logout time, login IP address, etc.

`lastb`. Same as `last`, except that by default it shows `/var/log/btmp`, which contains all the bad login attempts.

`lastlog`. This command reports data maintained in `/var/log/lastlog`, which is a record of the last time a user logged in.

`ac`. Available after installing the `acct` package. Prints the connect time in hours on a per-user basis or daily basis, etc. This command reads `/var/log/wtmp`.

`dump-utmp`. Converts raw data from /var/run/utmp or `/var/log/wtmp` into ASCII-parsable format.

Also check the `/var/log/messages` file, or the output of **journalctl** if no logging facility is running. See *Book "Administration Guide", Chapter 10 "*__journalctl__*: Query the* systemd *Journal"* for more information on the `systemd` journal.

### 3.32.3 Other

Finally, the following items are relevant to the system security as well, and misconfiguration can cause many problems – and should be reviewed:

- Resolver (`/etc/hosts`, `/etc/resolv.conf`, `/etc/nsswitch.conf`).

- NTP configuration (`/etc/ntp.conf`).

# A Documentation Updates

This chapter lists content changes for this document since the release of SUSE® Linux Enterprise Server 11 SP3.

This manual was updated on the following dates:

- Section A.1, "December 2015 (Initial Release of SUSE Linux Enterprise Server 12 SP1)"

- Section A.2, "February 2015 (Documentation Maintenance Update)"

- Section A.3, "October 2014 (Initial Release of SUSE Linux Enterprise Server 12)"

## A.1 December 2015 (Initial Release of SUSE Linux Enterprise Server 12 SP1)

**General**

- *Book "Subscription Management Tool for SLES 12 SP1"* is now part of the documentation for SUSE Linux Enterprise Server.

- Add-ons provided by SUSE have been renamed to modules and extensions. The manuals have been updated to reflect this change.

- Numerous small fixes and additions to the documentation, based on technical feedback.

- The registration service has been changed from Novell Customer Center to SUSE Customer Center.

- In YaST, you will now reach *Network Settings* via the *System* group. *Network Devices* is gone (https://bugzilla.suse.com/show_bug.cgi?id=867809).

- **Added** Section 3.14.4, "SUSE Manager" (Doc comment #26206).

- **Added** Section 3.9.12, " Filter access to /dev/mem (default in SUSE Linux Enterprise Server 12) " (Fate #315172).

**Bugfixes**

- Access to Removable Media Cannot be Restricted as Described (https://bugzilla.suse.com/show_bug.cgi?id=929918).

# A.2 February 2015 (Documentation Maintenance Update)

**Bugfixes**

- SLES hardening documentation wrong/incomplete—password strength (https://bugzilla.suse.com/show_bug.cgi?id=907754).

# A.3 October 2014 (Initial Release of SUSE Linux Enterprise Server 12)

**General**

- Removed all KDE documentation and references because KDE is no longer shipped.

- Removed all references to SuSEconfig, which is no longer supported (Fate #100011).

- Move from System V init to systemd (Fate #310421). Updated affected parts of the documentation.

- YaST Runlevel Editor has changed to Services Manager (Fate #312568). Updated affected parts of the documentation.

- Removed all references to ISDN support, as ISDN support has been removed (Fate #314594).

- Removed all references to the YaST DSL module as it is no longer shipped (Fate #316264).

- Removed all references to the YaST Modem module as it is no longer shipped (Fate #316264).

- Btrfs has become the default file system for the root partition (Fate #315901). Updated affected parts of the documentation.

- The **dmesg** now provides human-readable time stamps in `ctime()`-like format (Fate #316056). Updated affected parts of the documentation.

- syslog and syslog-ng have been replaced by rsyslog (Fate #316175). Updated affected parts of the documentation.

- MariaDB is now shipped as the relational database instead of MySQL (Fate #313595). Updated affected parts of the documentation.

- SUSE-related products are no longer available from http://download.novell.com but from http://download.suse.com. Adjusted links accordingly.

- Novell Customer Center has been replaced with SUSE Customer Center. Updated affected parts of the documentation.

- `/var/run` is mounted as tmpfs (Fate #303793). Updated affected parts of the documentation.

- The following architectures are no longer supported: Itanium and x86. Updated affected parts of the documentation.

- The traditional method for setting up the network with `ifconfig` has been replaced by `wicked`. Updated affected parts of the documentation.

- A lot of networking commands are deprecated and have been replaced by newer commands (usually **ip**). Updated affected parts of the documentation.

  ```
  arp: ip neighbor
  ifconfig: ip addr, ip link
  iptunnel: ip tunnel
  iwconfig: iw
  nameif: ip link, ifrename
  netstat: ss, ip route, ip -s link, ip maddr
  route: ip route
  ```

- Numerous small fixes and additions to the documentation, based on technical feedback.

*Section 3.5, "Retiring Linux Servers with Sensitive Data"*

- **Added** *Section 3.5.1, "scrub: Disk Overwrite Utility"* (Fate #315530).

*Section 3.9.9, "Virtual Address Space Randomization"*

- **Added** *Section 3.9.11, "Increased* `dmesg` *Restrictions"* (Fate #315175).

*Section 3.4, "Verifying Security Action with* `seccheck`*"*

- **Added** *Section 3.4.1, "Seccheck Configuration"* (Fate #312303).

## Obsolete Content

- 

## Bugfixes

- Removed all content about or references to ZENworks Linux Management.

www.ingramcontent.com/pod-product-compliance
Lightning Source LLC
Chambersburg PA
CBHW060458060326
40689CB00020B/4578